One Word From God
Can Change Your Family

D1132578

KENNETH
COPELAND
PUBLICATIONS

One Word From God Can Change Your Family

ISBN-10 1-57562-757-4   30-0711
ISBN-13 978-1-57562-757-1

19 18 17 16 15 14   17 16 15 14 13 12

© 1999 Kenneth and Gloria Copeland

Kenneth Copeland Publications
Fort Worth, TX 76192-0001

For more information about Kenneth Copeland Ministries, visit kcm. org or call 1-800-600-7395 (U.S. only) or +1-817-852-6000.

Contents

Introduction

One Word From God Can Change Your Life FOREVER!

When the revelation of this statement exploded on the inside of me, it changed the way I think...about everything! I had been praying for several days about a situation that seemed, at the time, to be overwhelming. I had been confessing the Word of God over it, but that Word had begun to come out of my head and not my heart. I was pushing in my flesh for the circumstance to change. As I made my confession one more time, the Spirit of God seemed to say to me, *Why don't you be quiet?!*

I said, "But Lord, I'm confessing the Word!"

He answered inside me, *I know it. I heard you. Now just be still and be quiet a little while, and let the Word of God settle down in your spirit. Quit trying to make this thing happen. You're not God. You're not going to be the one to make it happen anyway!*

So, I stopped. I stopped in that situation in my mind and began to get quiet before the Lord...and this phrase came up in my spirit..."**One** word from God can change anything."

So I started saying that. I said it off and on all day. It came easily because it came from God—not from my own thinking.

Every time I was tempted to worry or think of ideas concerning my circumstances, I'd think, *Yes, just one word from God...*

I noticed when I'd say that, **the peace of God** would come on me. It was so calming. As a result, a habit developed in me. People would bring me issues. They'd say, "Well, what about..." And I'd either say aloud or think to myself, **"Yeah, that may be so, but one word from God will change anything."**

It began to be the answer for everything. If I were watching television and the newscaster was telling about a disaster, and the people being interviewed were saying things to the effect of, "Oh, what are we going to do? It's all been blown away, burned up or shook up...," I'd say, **"Yeah, but one word from God can change anything."**

It really developed into a strength for me and it can for you. That's why we've put together the **One Word From God Book Series...**

there could be just one word in these inspiring articles that can change your family forever.

You've been searching, seeking help...and God has the answer. He has the one word that can turn your circumstance around and put you on dry ground. He has the one word that gives you all the peace that's in Him. He is your Father God. He wants you to have blessed, obedient children. He wants to increase your household more and more. He wants to establish His covenant with you and with your children after you (Genesis 9:9; Psalm 115:4; Proverbs 22:6).

God loves you. And He has a word for you. One Word that can change your life FOREVER!

Planting Hope in Our Kids

Chapter 1

Kenneth Copeland

"Behold, I will send you Elijah the prophet before the coming of the great and dreadful day of the Lord: And he shall turn the heart of the fathers to the children, and the heart of the children to their fathers, lest I come and smite the earth with a curse."

—MALACHI 4:5-6

Have you thought about the amount and kinds of imagery our children are having implanted into them by the world today? They are getting it on television and everywhere else—slick, high-tech, high-cost images of death and despair. They can't even walk up and down the streets today without having some kind of picture fed to them.

But that's changing. The time of *"Rachel weeping for her children"* (Jeremiah 31:15) is giving way to the time of hope: *"...for thy work shall be rewarded...and they shall come again from the land of the enemy. And there is hope in thine end, saith the Lord, that thy children shall come again to their own border"* (verses 16-17).

Head to Head With Hollywood

I've been in faith, praying and standing in expectancy for more than 20 years concerning revival among our children, and thank God, it's here. In early 1992, an outpouring of the Holy Ghost began on children and young people in this nation, and around the world.

This ministry is throwing its entire weight, effort, faith and strength into ministry to children just the same as we do our calling to teach adults. To accomplish this calling will take a lot. God told me it would. He said His people have been trying to use 29-cent quarterlies to compete with the technology of Disney, 20th Century Fox, Warner Brothers, ABC, CBS and NBC.

Maybe you've heard people talking about Christian material and products for children say something like, "Well that's good enough for kids." If so, think about this: The devil will spend $50 million on some horror movie every chance he gets—just to get our kids. He has spent the last 40 years, in particular, doing everything he can to totally destroy our children.

Hope Implants

But the kids need something the movie and entertainment industries are not giving them. They need what I call "hope implants." God implanted hope in Abraham by showing him the stars of the heavens to help him see how many children God was going to give him.

Like Abraham, children need a vision of hope. Hope is the image inside our hearts for which faith becomes the substance. Right now this is so far removed from the thinking of the children of this generation, that they could never grasp it if God didn't start it with a video or something powerfully graphic.

Children and young people of this day and time are totally immersed in imagery technology—high-tech sin, unbelief and ungodly material of every kind. Reading doesn't impress them much. In the younger ones, almost not at all. They are all image-dependent. Even their games are TV images. With God's power and wisdom, we can fill their hungry hearts and minds with images of God's grace, love and glory.

Malachi 4:5-6 says, *"Behold, I will send you Elijah the prophet before the coming of the great and dreadful day of the Lord: And he shall turn the heart of the fathers to the children, and the heart of the children to their fathers, lest I come and smite the earth with a curse."* It is significant that these are the last two verses of the Old Covenant.

Restoring Hearts

If God did not anoint the prophetic ministries in these end times to bring the hearts of the fathers to the children and the hearts of the children to the fathers, then the earth would be overwhelmed with a mighty curse.

But God is not going to allow that curse to take place. The anointing of Elijah, the double-portion kind of anointing of God Almighty, is restoring our children. It excites me because it is happening right now. That anointing has come and it's working! Praise God!

Children are coming to the Lord by the hundreds and the thousands and the tens of thousands all over the country, where people are reaching out to them and ministering to them. They're receiving hope! Their faith is coming alive!

Jesus Loves the Children

Jesus personally associated Himself with children. He told his disciples in Mark 10:13 to permit them to *"come unto me."*

Jesus instructs us to receive the kingdom of God as a little child. So, if we must become as a little child, why not get hold of a person when they *are* a little child?

Well, we're going at it. Whatever we must do, we're going to reach kids and give them hope. Our children's DVDs like *The Gunslinger, Treasure of Eagle Mountain* and *Covenant Rider* are a part of that. The *Commander Kellie and the Superkids*_{SM} DVDs like *The Intruder, Armor of Light* and *Judgment: The Trial of Commander Kellie* are part of that...and there'll be more to come. We're going at it, believing God. We're going at it, saying there is no price too big, no effort too great, no job too hard for our God to reach our children.

When God Says, "Pssst!"

Chapter 2

Gloria Copeland

"But the mercy of the Lord is from everlasting to everlasting upon them that fear him, and his righteousness unto children's children."
—Psalm 103:17

Did you know your children are in your heart? It's true. You carry your children in your heart the same way God carries you in His heart.

You can feel what's going on with them even when they're on the other side of the world. If they're hurt, if they're lonely, if they're toying with sin and getting off track—when things are wrong or things are right, you can feel it.

I remember once when Ken and I were in Australia. We were flying from one city to another and suddenly thoughts of our son, John, flooded my heart. John was a teenager at the time and he was all boy. He rode everything with wheels—cars, trucks, motorcycles, dune buggies. And it seemed he was always turning something over.

That day on the plane, I was concerned about him. I knew how much the devil would like to sneak in and steal his life, and I was concerned that John's misadventures could give the devil the opportunity to do it.

But the Holy Spirit broke in on my thoughts. He spoke to Ken and said, *My mercy hovers over John.* When Ken relayed those words to me, all my fears vanished.

My mercy hovers over John. I'll never forget that promise. As I've prayed for John throughout the years, that wonderful word from God would often rise up and remind me that John's life was secure. It would assure me that God would keep him and hold him steady until the day he got things straight in his life.

My mercy hovers over your child. That is a wonderful word from God. If God will do that for my child, He will do it for yours. The covenant God has made with you in the blood of Jesus extends to your children and your children's children. Psalm 103:17 says, *"But the mercy of the Lord is from everlasting to everlasting upon them that fear him, and his righteousness unto children's children."*

Our grandchildren are covered in our covenant

with God. Everything God gives to me, He'll give to them. All the protection I have, He passes on to my family.

If you're a believer and willing to trust God for the deliverance and salvation of your children, you'll not be disappointed.

Study Zechariah 10:7-9. There, God tells us about the outpouring of the Spirit of God in the last days—the days we're living in. He says:

> **And they of Ephraim shall be like a mighty man, and their heart shall rejoice as through wine: yea, their children shall see it, and be glad; their heart shall rejoice in the Lord. I will hiss for them [your children], and gather them; for I have redeemed them.... And I will sow them among the people: and they shall remember me in far countries; and they shall live with their children, and turn again.**

You may not even know where your children are right now. They may be in another city or another country. It doesn't matter. This scripture says when you rejoice in the Lord—not when you're depressed or worried or afraid, but when you trust God so totally that you're filled up with joy—then your children will see it and turn.

"I will hiss for them." What does that mean? It means God will signal for them. He'll say, *Pssst! Come here!* And they'll come running.

Let me tell you something. God knows how to get someone's attention. He knows how to signal for the ones His people are praying for. Kenneth's mother prayed for me and then one day God said, *Pssst, Gloria!* I heard Him and was born again.

I didn't know much about God before that time. I knew there was a God, but had no real knowledge about Him. Yet, He still knew how to get my attention. He called and here I am today preaching His Word!

He'll do the same thing for your child. It doesn't matter what kind of wickedness that child has fallen into, God can still reach him. I know a man who pastors a great church in Sacramento, California. His name is Phil Goudeaux. He used to be part of the militant black power movement. In fact, he was in charge of security for the Black Panthers.

He didn't know God and he didn't want to know God. But one day when he was in college, a young, white fellow came over to his lunch table and started telling him about Jesus. This Black Panther leader couldn't believe it. The nerve of this guy! He tried to get rid of him. He threatened him and even tried to hit him...but he couldn't.

For weeks this little, white fellow followed this big, "bad" black guy around talking to him about Jesus. Finally, the Black Panther prayed with the fellow just to get him off his back. After that he tried to forget about it...but he couldn't. Two weeks later, all by himself, he made Jesus Christ the Lord of his life.

God knows how to get someone's attention! He'll knock them over and speak to them right out loud if He needs to. He proved that in the life of a man named Saul. Years after that man was saved, he wrote, *"...I follow after, if that I may apprehend that for which also I am apprehended of Christ Jesus"* (Philippians 3:12).

God apprehended Paul one day on the road to Damascus. According to the dictionary, to *apprehend* means "to capture" or "arrest." God captured Paul's attention. The last thing he wanted to be was a follower of Jesus. He was a declared enemy of Jesus. But God was able to apprehend him anyway.

Don't you worry. God knows exactly how to apprehend your children. And when the time comes, He'll do it. After all, you weren't in your prayer closet when He found you!

But, until then, you must stand fast in faith for them. No matter what they get into, no matter how far off the track they seem to be, just keep saying what the Bible says about them. Keep your eyes focused on the covenant mercy of God and not on the symptoms of ungodliness that you see in their lives.

Don't ever give up on your child. If you've grown weak and discouraged lately, it's time for you to get that fire back in your bones. Dig into the Word of God and dig out the promises He's given you for your children. Lay hold of those promises and don't let go.

Learn to call things that are not as though they were (Romans 4:17). When you hear bad news about your children or you see them do something that hurts your heart, just say: "God, I thank You that Your tender mercy hovers over my child. I thank You, Lord, that he is born again, filled with the Holy Ghost and obedient to You. I thank You that Your Word is in his mouth (Isaiah 59:21), that he is taught by Your Spirit and great is his peace (Isaiah 54:13). I am not moved by what I feel or what I see. I am moved by Your Word and I call it done in Jesus' Name!"

I'm going to say it one more time: You have a covenant with God that covers your children. So rejoice! God will be faithful to you. One day your boy or your girl will be going about their business doing their own thing when suddenly— *Pssst!*—they'll hear the voice of God.

When that happens, they'll come running.

You can count on it.

Chapter 3

Training Your Child to Make the Right Choices

Vikki Burke

"Train up a child in the way he should go: and when he is old, he will not depart from it."
—PROVERBS 22:6

The episode is embarrassing—and familiar. You've witnessed this scene just like I have: A child is screaming and kicking on the floor, pointing to candy bars at the checkout stand. The mother, ignoring the entire situation, hurriedly writes her check for the groceries.

What's the matter with her? you wonder. *Can't she control her child?* Maybe not—especially if she doesn't know how to train the will of her child. The challenge before that mother is one every parent must encounter: How do I train my child to make the right decisions that will help him in life—and not harm him?

Relief Is Here!

The answer is within reach! You have someone to pattern your parenting after, and it isn't Dr. Spock! It's God, who is worthy of imitation. Ephesians 3:14-15 says, *"For this reason, I bow my knees before the Father, from whom every family in heaven and on earth derives its name" (New American Standard).* Since God is your model for parenting, you don't have to control your child any more than your heavenly Father controls you. What good news!

"But, Vikki, are you saying I'm supposed to just turn my child loose to do whatever he wants?"

No. Your role is to train the will of your child so he will learn how to make choices that are consistent with God's purpose for him. Let's look at six things you can begin doing today that will help pump up your parental influence—actions and attitudes that will let you help your child set the course for his destiny in God.

1. Respect the Bent

Your influence as a parent begins with discovering God's plan for your child—a plan indicated by the individual gift, or bent, in his life. A very familiar verse translated in *The Amplified Bible* says, *"Train up a child in the way he should go*

*[and in keeping with his individual gift or bent],
and when he is old he will not depart from it"*
(Proverbs 22:6).

A gift is a natural endowment, aptitude or
talent. A bent is a personal inclination, a strong
liking or favor for something. Knowing your
child's aptitudes and inclinations, you can
understand the motivations for his actions and
help direct your child into God's purposes for
his life.

This is much more important than making
him conform to some image you may have for
his future. I have heard parents say of a
newborn, "My son is going to be a prophet."
That's wonderful if God has called him to that,
but if He hasn't, they are manipulating, instead
of influencing. When parents impose their own
desires on a child, it becomes control.

You cannot confess gifts and callings on
another person—even your own child. It's God's
purposes, not yours, that you want to help your
child discover. To do this, first, seek God for His
plan and second, keep with or follow that plan
in the way you influence your child.

2. Help Him Value Right Choices

The only way the true character of your child, or anyone else, can be revealed, is through the exercise of his will, through freedom of choice. This is by God's design. For your child to learn to make right choices, he must exercise the privilege and responsibility of freedom of choice.

God did not make man to be controlled or oppressed, and He never forces a decision on anyone. Look at how God presented the blessings of His covenant to His people: *"See, I have set before you today life and prosperity, and death and adversity"* (Deuteronomy 30:15, *New American Standard*). He always leaves the final choice to man.

If the freedom of His children to make their own choices is important to God, it should be no less important to you as a parent. If you force your child's choices, you are controlling him. Instead, show him what a tremendous gift and responsibility his freedom to choose is. Let him know that the final responsibility of the choices he makes (and the consequences of those choices!) always remains with him, and not with you as his parent.

Breaking your child's will is not the goal. When talking about the will here, I am referring to decision-making, or choosing between two possible actions.

The thought that parents are to break the will of their child goes totally against the character of God. Breaking the will forces an action against one's choice, which always results in resentment, bitterness and rebellion. A child with a broken will is not equipped to face the challenges of adulthood, nor will he have the power to sustain the attacks of the world.

Learning to express his will through freedom of choice is an essential part of growing up. For your child to confidently and consistently decide the right action, he must have his will trained—not broken.

3. Help Him Understand Consequences

Though you are not to control his choices, you do have the right, and the assignment, to influence your child in how to recognize and make the right choices. To influence means to "produce an effect upon the actions or thoughts of, to persuade, to mold, to modify." You sway your child to make a decision or to go in a certain direction, persuade him to adopt a view or begin an action, and mold his character. The scriptural goal of discipline is to persuade (induce or convince) to a belief.

In God's system, freedom to choose is always followed by consequences of those choices (Deuteronomy 30:15). God makes the outcome clear, in advance, but the decision is up to the individual.

Let your child know not only his options, but also the consequences of each possible decision. Clearly and consistently state the rules and boundaries. This is the only way he can be certain of what you expect and be secure about his actions and your reactions.

What should you do if your child refuses to comply with your request? Persuade him to be influenced the next time! If your child refuses to cooperate, simply respond, "It is your choice to obey or disobey. You can do what I have asked or receive the penalty for your disobedience."

This places the power in his hand and gives him a new decision to make. Once again, he is free to make a choice. If he continues in disobedience, he must receive the penalty—

whatever discipline you feel is appropriate. When discipline has been completed, both parent and child are released to begin anew with the next decision. In this manner, punishment and penalty are clearly linked to his choice, not to the issue and not to the parent enforcing the penalty.

Remember, you will not change a child's will by anger or force, but by gentle encouragement to a wiser, more excellent choice. It's by the goodness or kindness of God that men are led to repentance—not by harshness or control (Romans 2:4). To arouse children emotionally, such as with threats, will only frustrate the process of persuasion. Instead, set before them the standard of the Word of God and let it sway them.

4. *Make the Love Connection*

You may be asking what it takes to have this kind of influence in guiding your child. Remember, God is your pattern, and He doesn't parent by dictatorship, but by relationship.

A relationship is a connection between two people. When a connection is made, there is a flow of power, just like electricity. Some parents never make that connection. They never create the bonds that let love flow easily to and from their children.

You and your son or daughter need to make contact with one another. This is more than being in the same room. It is a flowing, joining and bonding together. Ruling with absolute power does not form this kind of bond. Sooner or later, dictatorship always results in rebellion. The kind of bonding that will hold you together when things get tough doesn't stop at birth, but is a process that continues for life, cementing the two of you and making you both strong.

5. Demonstrate Integrity

The strength of this bond demands integrity. The children of this generation are looking for something real. They're crying out for something with power, something that will put them over. And they're experts at spotting a fake. Don't try to lift a standard before your son or daughter by which you are not willing to live.

The hypocritical words, "Do as I say, not as I do," are powerless. If you continually make demands on your child that you are unwilling to fulfill yourself, he will rebel. I heard someone put it this way: "Rules without relationship create rebellion." He needs you to be a living, walking demonstration that the *"commandment which I command you today is not too difficult for you, nor is it out of reach"* (Deuteronomy 30:11, *New American Standard*).

This may require you to make some adjustments in your life—but that's good. One of the greatest functions of the Holy Spirit is His guidance. He'll show you how to get on track and away from snares and pitfalls.

All of us are familiar with gravitational pull. It's what causes the Earth and other planets to stay in rotation around the sun, and our feet to stay planted on Earth. Truly living by the standard God sets before you as a believer, also creates a gravitational pull. It will cause your children to gravitate toward you and toward the Lord Jesus. People draw toward what is real and genuine.

6. *Esteem the Child*

To give respect, your child must be shown respect. The commandment to honor father and mother is given to children with the promise of a long life, full of blessing (Ephesians 6:2-3). But if your child doesn't receive honor and respect in the home, he will not give it to you in return—or anyone else.

Remember Luke 6:38: *"Give, and it will be given to you.... For by your standard of measure it will be measured to you in return"* *(New American Standard).* Money is not the only issue here. If you were raised with honor and respect, you will give it to your child. If you were raised with criticism, that's what you will give, unless you break its power and replace it with honor and respect.

Honoring your child is not difficult—merely regard or esteem him as God's child. This does not mean that he rules the house, or has the right to interrupt at any time, or behave without proper discipline. It means you give him recognition and treat him with respect and courtesy.

See your child as God sees him...with pleasure, affection and approval. One way you show your esteem for your child is by showing your desire to spend time with him like God showed his desire to have fellowship with Adam in the Garden of Eden. God desired to dwell among His people.

(See Exodus 25:8, 29:42-46.) But He wasn't satisfied with simply dwelling among them. He sent His own Spirit to dwell in His people (1 John 4:13). His desire is to be close—so close He lives within every child of God.

Don't forget, that however you view your child, he will sense it, and it will become the way in which he esteems himself—both in your family and God's.

Mirrors of God's Glory

Adam's purpose was to reflect the glory of God. God wanted to demonstrate His holiness, love, wisdom, comfort, faithfulness and grace through him. Man is to be the reflection of God's character.

It shouldn't surprise us, then, that God has given children the inborn desire to imitate their parents. Every child has said, "I want to be like my daddy (or mommy) when I grow up."

That's one reason they crave fellowship with you more than anything else that could be offered to them. They want to be near you, to spend time with you. When children from 5 to 18 years old were asked by a television host, "If you could have anything in the world from your parents, what would it be?" they all answered essentially the same way: "I would like to spend time with my parents." A relationship with their parents is necessary to helping them feel accepted and approved.

This inborn desire gives you a great opportunity—an opportunity to guide them in their choices, rather than to control them. Like a mirror, your children will reflect your life. If you have patterned your parenting after God, they will manifest the values you display and be reflections of God's glory.

Show them that their freedom of choice is a gift to be valued and protected. Help them appreciate the privilege and responsibility of that freedom. Build the bond and the connection that lets love flow freely between you. Then watch as the choices they make lead them into fulfillment of their destiny in God.

Chapter 4

Influencing Your Children for God

Willie George

"For I know him, that he will command his children and his household after him, and they shall keep the way of the Lord, to do justice and judgment; that the Lord may bring upon Abraham that which he hath spoken of him."
—GENESIS 18:19

In my camp-meeting ministry to thousands of children through the years, one thing has continued to amaze me. It is the number of older children—12-year-olds, raised in church, whose parents are active in church—who do not receive Jesus until those meetings.

I often wonder, *Why wasn't that kid saved before he got here? What's been going on?*

Many, many parents in the kingdom of God love God and want to serve Him, but they do not train their own kids. Some moms and dads, just because they have the things of God, assume that their kids will somehow get those things on their own. Other parents are not confident that they can train their kids in the way that they should go.

But, successful parenting in troubled times requires that parents are personally and actively involved in training their children. Children need the kind of influence demonstrated by Abraham, who is singled out as an example of a godly parent.

Caring Enough to Command

In Genesis 18:17-19, the Lord said, *"...Shall I hide from Abraham that thing which I do; Seeing that Abraham shall surely become a great and mighty nation, and all the nations of the earth shall be blessed in him? For I know him, that he will command his children and his household after him, and they shall keep the way of the Lord, to do justice and judgment...."*

God said He chose Abraham because he would *"command his children and his household after him."* The whole process of child training focuses on taking your children, making decisions for them and as they get a little older, pulling back a little bit to allow them to make decisions on their own. If you will do this, by the time they are grown, they will have made so many decisions, they will know how to handle things like money, sex, rebellion, drugs and temptation—all the things that pressure them in the world.

Commanding your children means making decisions for them that they are not ready to make. It requires you to exercise your authority as a parent.

When I was younger, I lived with my uncle, who was a pastor. He once told me about a family in which the mother would not allow the father to discipline the children, including an older son who was 17.

This woman was against smoking, movies, whiskey, drinking and dancing, but she had a tongue about a mile long. She was always criticizing my uncle, the pastor, and planting seeds of discord in the church. At the same time, this woman could not control her children.

Finally, my uncle said to her, "You need to watch your step. You curse me and come against me and speak evil against me, but if you don't train and discipline those children and start listening to what I'm trying to teach you, the day is coming when your own son will curse you to your face."

"It will never happen," she said. But less than a year later, the 17-year-old came home drunk one night. His mom caught him and when she confronted him, he just cursed her to her face.

She was not a successful parent. She did not command her children. As a parent, you have to make up your mind right now that there are a lot of things you'll have to do because you know to do them, and not because you feel like doing them.

Abraham commanded his children and his household, even when it didn't feel good. In Genesis 21:8-12, Ishmael, Abraham's teenage son by Sarah's handmaid Hagar, was caught mocking his younger half-brother Isaac—the heir of God's promises. Scripture says to think about sending Hagar and Ishmael away was *"very grievous in Abraham's sight."* But Abraham could see how growing up with an older brother continually dogging him and cutting him down would not be good for Isaac.

Now today, you can't cast out older children when they hurt the little ones. But if you have anybody living in your home, they should abide by your rules. Abraham was not the kind of man to say, "Whatever you want to do, do it." He was a man of authority. He said, "If you're living here and I am paying the bills, you're going to abide by my rules." When he was circumcised, every man in his household was circumcised. He commanded not only his children, but his household to keep the way of the Lord.

Know What They're Exposed To

Another responsibility you have in influencing your children is to know what your children are exposed to. There was a great difference in Abraham and his grandson Jacob in this matter.

Genesis 24 tells us that when Isaac was a young man, Abraham sent his servant back to the land of his people to find a bride for Isaac so he would not marry a Canaanite woman.

But Jacob was careless about what he let his children be exposed to. According to Genesis 34:1-2, "...*Dinah the daughter of Leah, which she bare unto Jacob, went out to see the daughters of the land. And when Shechem the son of Hamor the Hivite, prince of the country, saw her, he took her, and lay with her, and defiled her.*"

The Canaanites were a wicked, immoral, ungodly people who worshiped devils and practiced witchcraft. Jacob allowed his daughter to go out, without any supervision, to meet the daughters in the land of Canaan. Because of his carelessness and failure to teach his kids, Dinah stepped out of protection and was harmed.

"Well, I thought Jacob had God's protection. He was from the seed of Abraham," you may say.

Yes, he was the seed of Abraham, but he failed to teach and influence his children for God. He didn't look out for them.

In the same way, you need to know where your kids are and what they're doing. You need to know who their friends are. You should be very aware of what's going on in their lives.

Several years ago I had a secretary who prayed for her little girls all day, every day. But one time, despite the fact that she had a check in her spirit, she let one of them spend the night with a friend next door. All night long the mother was burdened to pray in the Spirit for her daughter. Early the next morning, she learned that the neighbor's 10-year-old son had tried to molest her daughter.

You can't assume anything about another family. We like to have the kids our children are playing with come in the house every now and then. That way we can meet them and look them in the eye and discern what kinds of spirits these kids have before we allow our children to continue playing with them.

There is one group of kids in our neighborhood we do not allow our children to play with. Although they are from a church-going family of professing Christians, a terrible spirit of strife follows the children wherever they go. When they are with our children, they try to turn our boys against each other or against their little sister. We finally had to tell this family, "You keep your kids at home."

Not only do you need to know to whom your children are exposed, but also to what they are exposed. When our boys were younger, they bought little action figures from a certain television series before we had checked it out carefully. When I read the book that came with the figures, I saw the phrase, "We call the spirits into our bodies and they came into us and they changed us."

They were talking about inviting demons

into their bodies! You can call it play-like and fantasy all you want to, but that type of imagery is a very real thing. You just don't play with those things.

Never Quit Praying

There may come a time, as your children grow into their teenage years, when your influence may not seem very great. Even if you can't influence your kids, don't assume that no one can. God can repackage His message and send it to them in another vehicle.

My own parents never really had any godly influence over me, but every time I went to Grandma's house, she'd talk to me about the things of God and really preach at me and tell me I ought to be in Sunday school. I didn't listen to my grandmother, and finally she just gave up talking to me about it. But the one thing she didn't give up was praying and believing God for me.

Then, when I was 17, God allowed some

things to happen in my life that made me just sick of the world. I began to get fed up with the hypocrisy I saw in my friends and the way people used people.

When evangelist James Robison came to my high school about three weeks after that, I was ready to get saved. That happened because of my grandmother's prayers. Although her influence on me had totally dropped, she never lost her influence with God.

Don't ever give up being involved in the lives of your children. God will show you how to train them in the way that they should go. Make the decision to exercise godly authority in love for them, even when it is not pleasant to do so. Decide that you are going to know what they are exposed to.

God likes to make covenants with parents who, like Abraham, are careful what influences they allow on their children. The blessings He promised to Abraham belong to parents who will make the right decisions about their kids— who will command their children. You can influence your children for God.

God Is No Respecter

Chapter 5

Marty Copeland

"And Jesus answering saith unto them, Have faith in God. For verily I say unto you, That whosoever shall say unto this mountain, Be thou removed, and be thou cast into the sea; and shall not doubt in his heart, but shall believe that those things which he saith shall come to pass; he shall have whatsoever he saith. Therefore I say unto you, What things soever ye desire, when ye pray, believe that ye receive them, and ye shall have them."

—MARK 11:22-24

Keeping a husband and wife from having children is one of the most devastating things Satan can do to a couple. It is also one of the toughest faith battles you can fight because it involves you, your spouse, your child, and specifically the call of God on the life of the child He has promised you.

For three years John and I dealt with child-lessness. We dealt with the thoughts that arose when well-meaning friends or relatives asked, "Well, how come you aren't pregnant?... I thought you all were going to get pregnant last year. Why don't you have a baby yet?"

At one point, I remember feeling I wasn't a "whole woman" because I couldn't give my husband the blessing of a child... (wrong thinking, huh?).

But John, because of the way he was raised, just didn't operate in fear or doubt. And I had no problem believing God for healing because of the teaching I had been exposed to, and because He had healed me of things before. Nonetheless, focus on the physical healing I needed to be able to conceive, the waiting, doctors' opinions and discouragement all took a toll on my faith.

By the West Coast Believers' Convention in Anaheim, California, in 1991, I was becoming discouraged. But that year, Kenneth prophesied over me: *"Because of your faith, the Word has taken root in you, and it won't be too much longer."*

John and I knew that it was God Who had placed in us the desire to have a family. Truly believing we received, we confessed God's promise and thanked Him for it daily. Every time we prayed over our food, John and I would say aloud, "Father, I thank You that Marty's pregnant. We have a perfect child."

I continued to let God show me new ways to sow seeds for the specific things I was believing for. I gave a baby shower to honor and bless a friend, but knew I was sowing into my harvest as well. I made a conscious decision to sow more love into the lives of the children around me.

Despite all of this, I needed a breakthrough. When I asked God what was wrong, His answer was not a formula. It was not that I was "missing it." It was that I wasn't seeking Him enough. I wasn't pressing in with my faith in every area possible. I had only focused my faith in the area of healing, and because of the discouragement, I was beginning to waver.

Shortly after Kenneth prophesied to me, my turnaround came. God gave John's grandmother a word for me—the story of Hannah being delivered from childlessness to give birth to Samuel (1 Samuel 1).

While I was already standing on many scriptures, this revelation particularly ministered to me. Daily, as I read Hannah's story and prayed her prayer, the revelation grew stronger in me that God is no respecter of persons. I got mad at the devil. I stayed in his face with the fact that God loved me as much as He loved Hannah. I repeatedly said aloud that if God would do that for Hannah, He'll do it for me. I said of friends who had conceived, if God would do that for her, He'll do it for me. And I thanked Him and praised Him for it.

God met me where I was. I no longer focused entirely on healing for my body, but on the reality that God is no respecter of persons. Daily, my faith grew stronger.

Within two months I was pregnant. On April 7, 1992, Courtney was born. John, who had encouraged me through every bad report, spoke the same words he had confessed at every meal: "She's perfect."

Continuing to believe for a child is truly a faith battle, whether you have waited three years or 10. It's not easy, and is often emotionally painful. If you are wrestling with this and you're doing all you know to do, then regroup. Look for new areas to apply your faith. God will meet you where you are and take up any slack necessary for you to receive your manifestation.

Children are the right of a marriage in

covenant with God (Deuteronomy 28:11), and God is no respecter of persons. What He has done for others, He will surely do for you.

Chapter 6

A Force to Be Reckoned With

"Now no chastening for the present seemeth to be joyous, but grievous: nevertheless afterward it yieldeth the peaceable fruit of righteousness unto them which are exercised thereby."
—HEBREWS 12:11

I'm an Australian, and I love the United States. One thing I've noticed about these two countries is the special bond they have had in times of conflict. American soldiers even like to fight alongside Australians—because they're good.

There's a reason Australian troops are considered some of the best soldiers in the world. The government of Australia puts them through extensive training. And because of their training, they know exactly what to do when pressure comes. Proper training makes those soldiers a force to be reckoned with. Without it, they would lose the battle, and their lives.

But the training those soldiers receive is no more important than the training that you, as parents, give your children. You have a choice to make with them. You can send them out into life without training, and see them torn apart by the pressures of life, or, you can train them well, and see them respond instantly and correctly to those pressures. You can see them rise up to become a force to be reckoned with.

The very lives of our young people can depend on whether or not they have been trained to hear God's voice and obey Him promptly and completely. That's why my heart breaks when I minister to young people. They are being given everything except the most important thing—training in how to make right decisions. So many of them are not getting the kind of training we read about in Hebrews 12:11: *"For the time being no discipline brings joy but seems grievous and painful, but afterwards it yields a peaceable fruit of righteousness to those who have been trained by it—a harvest of fruit which consists in righteousness, [that is, in conformity to God's will in purpose, thought and action, resulting in right living and right standing with God]"* (The Amplified Bible).

The reason training in God's Word is so important is that in a time of pressure, your child will react exactly as he or she has been trained. Think about it. Are you raising your child on, "Whatever you think, Darlin'," or are you teaching her to be confident in God's love for her, to hear His voice and to respond to Him without question?

How you answer that question will determine, for instance, what your teenage daughter will do when a young man from the world is trying to hassle her. What will she do? She's going to do what you have trained her to do. If you have raised her to be confident in God's love for her, to hear His voice and respond to Him without question, that's what she will do. She'll be a force to be reckoned with.

Trained to Value Correction

Where do you start training your children to be world-overcoming vessels of God's anointing in this earth? You start by giving them positive, Bible correction early in life. Proverbs 13:24 in *The Amplified Bible* says, "...he who loves [his son] diligently disciplines and punishes him early."

Starting early is the way you get them past the point of *"for the time being no discipline brings joy but seems grievous and painful..."*

and on to the place where they can learn to value proper correction as a benefit to them.

A child will not suddenly submit to the rod when he's 15. That doesn't mean to give up if your teenager hasn't already been taught to value proper correction. Pray for him. Remember that there is certainly now no condemnation to those who are in Christ Jesus, and all things are possible to them that believe. But realize you can't force a child to value correction if that child has not grown up seeing it ministered consistently and in love.

One of the great deceptions many parents have is that children have to go through a stage of rebellion. They say, "I'm not looking forward to my children becoming teenagers, because I know they're going to rebel, like all the others at that age."

If you keep saying that, they will. But if you will start correction early, your children can go on through their teenage years and into young adulthood without turning from God's Word.

From their earliest years, I have trained and corrected my boys, believing that they won't rebel. I pray that they will keep themselves pure, strong and healthy. I pray now they'll never depart from the Lord, that they'll think it's strange that people aren't Christians.

I grew up under that kind of praying and training. I was trained to love the Lord and to seek His decision first before anyone else's. And I never rebelled against God's Word.

That doesn't mean I didn't have some challenges in dealing with worldly authorities in my life. When I was 18, I had a teacher who was teaching evolution. He knew I was a minister's son and a Christian, and he would try to use the Bible to prove his point. He and the class would ridicule me for not believing in evolution. When they did, I just laughed at them.

I've had pressure put on me from the world. But when that outward pressure came, my training kept me from the kind of inner pressure to doubt God and compromise His Word.

It never occurred to me to seek the world's opinion. I thought the world's opinions stunk and was never embarrassed to say so. I was a force to be reckoned with because I learned early what true obedience was and that correction was good for me.

Trained in True Obedience

Training a child early includes teaching them what true, Bible obedience is. By teaching them to obey you promptly and without question, you are teaching them to trust and obey God Who cares for them and wants the very best for them.

Training a child in true obedience will include teaching him to obey when he doesn't feel like it. Have you ever heard of a sergeant who asked his men, "All right, you little blessings, would you please get out of bed now?" No, that sergeant demands immediate, unquestioning obedience.

Why? Because in combat, those soldiers will automatically do what they're trained to do.

True obedience means teaching your child to obey unconditionally. Your children need to learn to respond to your voice in the same way those soldiers respond to their sergeant. They need to learn to obey for the sake of obedience.

That means they need to learn true obedience isn't bought through bribes of money, gifts or favors. True obedience isn't doing something because of what they think they'll get out of it, but because it's right and expected (Ephesians 6:1). Teach them that to *"obey your parents in all things...is well pleasing to the Lord"* (Colossians 3:20, *New King James Version).*

Bribes will only teach them to try to bargain with God. You don't want them growing up telling Him, "I'll do this if You'll do that." God doesn't bribe His children. He wants them to obey Him because they love Him, not because of what they're going to get.

True obedience also means to obey completely and wholeheartedly. Children want to do just what is necessary—then quit. For instance, it takes proper training for them to see that cleaning up after dinner doesn't mean just doing the dishes in the sink. It means cleaning the sink, wiping all the table and countertops, and putting away the tea towels.

Take the time to show them how to do the job right. Show them what a completed job involves, and make sure they understand that partial obedience is really disobedience.

Finally, true obedience means to obey promptly. Prompt obedience is the way you train your children to hear God's voice. Your children should be trained to obey the first time you ask them to do something in your normal tone of voice. As they learn to respond to simple directions when they're young, their hearts will be prepared to obey the Lord in more important areas when they're older.

Your primary responsibility as a parent, is to develop the character of your children. As they grow to value obedience for the sake of obedience, they will begin to experience God's favor. Their strength of character, coupled with God's favor, will help them make a difference as young men and women in our world.

A Force for Faith

The child trained to trust God unconditionally will grow into a person who can boldly turn the pressures of the world into opportunities for faith. And those pressures will come.

I was asked to speak in an Australian city to the members of a popular civic club. The challenge I faced was that the members of that particular club had a reputation for drinking, ridiculing and even shouting out obscenities as their guest speakers spoke. I agreed, on the condition they would not identify the speaker as a minister, but as president of Daystar International, Ltd. (Daystar International, Ltd. incorporates Daystar Family Church where I am pastor, and Daystar International Bible Training College).

As the day came, a member of the club called, concerned about me and wondering whether I should speak after all.

"No, I need to speak," I said. "You haven't told them I'm a minister, have you?"

"Well, no," he said, "But, Ian, they're going to be foul and I don't know whether I...."

"It's all right," I assured him.

At the head table the next day, I watched as the booze began to flow and the smoke got so thick at times I could hardly see the audience. When they introduced me, everybody settled back, beers in hands and faces etched with curiosity—"Who we gonna eat tonight?"

"My name's Ian Britza and I'm the president of Daystar International, Ltd."

Some bloke yelled out, "What business is that?"

"I'm in the business of looking after the

spiritual state of our community," I said.

I noticed a couple of sneers.

"There's one thing that I can't stand and that's a cynic," I said. "Cynics are people who show everybody how ignorant they are.

"When I was 7 years old, God—whether you believe in God or not is beside the point— God spoke to me. He said I was going to be called to look after the spiritual state of people, to be a minister. I know you people don't go to church. It's a shame, because when you're in trouble, it's the minister you look to for help. It's me you come to. Whether you like it or agree with it or not, it's me."

You could have heard a pin drop.

"So don't come to me and ridicule my office when I've given my whole life, 24 hours a day," I continued. "You clock out at 5 o'clock. I don't clock out. I care about your families. I care about the needs of your young people, your teenagers. I've committed my life to speak to them whenever they have a problem. My community needs me in this city."

That's the way I spoke for about 25 or 30 minutes. There was absolute silence. When it came time for questions, no one said, "Boo." The president stood up and said, "I've never heard anything like this in my life." And men came up to me and said, "I just really appreciate that."

I didn't try to get that response. I just responded to the training I had received as a child. Sometimes we bring our children up to almost apologize for being a Christian. I didn't apologize for my Christianity because I had been trained to know that my parents love me. I was trained to know that God loves me. And that gave me great security—the security to jump out and say what God knew those men needed to hear.

Some people misunderstand that and say, "Oh, man of faith, you walk on water." No, no, no, no. I walk on water because I have great faith in the One Who loves me.

And it's not an effort, people. Don't put men like Dr. Lester Sumrall, or Kenneth Hagin, or Kenneth Copeland on some kind of unreachable pedestal. The reason they walk in faith so consistently and effortlessly is because they know that their heavenly Father loves them. They've trained themselves to respond to Him instantly and confidently.

That's how we are to raise our children. Through proper correction, we train our children's hearts to follow God's will for them. Then they will know the joy and peace that comes from confident, uncompromising obedience to His voice. As they grow, they won't rebel or be overcome by the world. Instead, they'll be a force to be reckoned with.

Chapter 7

Men, Join the Fatherhood Revolution!

Dennis Burke

"The just man walketh in his integrity: his children are blessed after him."
—PROVERBS 20:7

We are in the middle of a revolution—a revolution of fatherhood. A revolution to bring the power of godly leadership and manhood back into the hands of godly fathers.

It's the cry of our day—for men who will stand up and be men in their own homes. Men, whose focus is not the corporate ladder or the golf course. Men, whose hearts are turned toward their families.

In 1989 the Holy Spirit spoke to me and said, *There is going to be a revival of fatherhood in the land. It will take place in natural fathers as well as spiritual fathers. They will begin to take on the role of being fathers to their children.*

Immediately, I began to seek God regarding my own role as a father. As I did, I saw that there was a real deficit in fatherhood in our land. According to one study, the average father spends less than one minute a day of meaningful, uninterrupted time with each of his children. Another study concluded that more than 26 percent of the children in America are living in single-parent homes—the majority with their mothers.

Statistics like this make one thing obvious: The success of a man has been rated by everything except by taking on the real responsibility of fatherhood. Some of the most lauded businessmen, and even ministers, have suffered tragic failure in their families. Families everywhere are crying out for desperately needed guidance and direction from the dads. In the absence of that input, mothers have been burdened with much of the role of fatherhood. Often the mom is the only parent who gives any meaningful, spiritual input into the family.

Obviously, real fatherhood is much more than just providing financially for the family. *Webster's Third New International Dictionary* tells us *fatherhood* is "godhood in the paternal aspect."

The Bible describes the father as one who is to the family what God is to the Body of

Christ. Some of the things God is to believers includes provider, teacher, guide, comforter, counselor and strengthener. A father is to represent these roles to his family as he imitates and is empowered by the fatherhood of God.

To do this successfully, a real father should look for every opportunity to instill in his children the qualities and values that will help sustain and direct them to God. He should train them according to the Word of God, as Ephesians 6:4 instructs, *"Fathers, don't over-correct your children or make it difficult for them to obey the commandment. Bring them up with Christian teaching in Christian discipline"* (J.B. Phillips Translation).

The Anointing for Fatherhood

One of the real joys of the day we live in is that God has provided an empowering for fatherhood like the world has never seen. This anointing for fatherhood was prophesied in the very last words of the Old Testament: *"Behold, I will send you Elijah the prophet before the coming of the great and dreadful day of the Lord: And he shall turn the heart of the fathers to the children, and the heart of the children to their fathers, lest I come and smite the earth with a curse"* (Malachi 4:5-6).

That prophecy links the revival of fatherhood directly to the move of God in preparing the way for the return of the Lord. This is good news! In this last-days' outpouring of God's Spirit, there is an anointing for us to be the kind of fathers God has created us to be.

To enter in to this anointing, first understand that this revolution of fatherhood does not begin in you. True fatherhood begins in the heart of God. All authority and importance associated with fatherhood on earth derives from the divine fatherhood of God in heaven. Ephesians 3:14-15 says, *"For this cause I bow my knees unto the Father of our Lord Jesus Christ, of whom the whole family in heaven and earth is named."* The *Twentieth Century New Testament* translation of verse 15 reads, *"from whom all 'fatherhood' in Heaven and on earth derives its name."*

Jesus showed us God as a Father of love. He showed us the real heart that God wants to develop within every one of us—a heart turned toward our children. That's the heart Abraham had. God said His reason for making covenant with Abraham was because *"I know him, that he will command his children and his household after him, and they shall keep the way of the Lord, to do justice and judgment; that the Lord may bring upon Abraham that which he hath spoken of him"* (Genesis 18:19).

Abraham did instill in his children—and they in their children—the desire to keep the way of the Lord. And God's promises to them were fulfilled as they followed His ways. Because of this, when God spoke to Moses years later, He identified Himself, not just as the God of Abraham, but the God of Abraham, Isaac and Jacob.

We, like Abraham, can create in our children a desire to keep the way of the Lord. By expressing the heart of Father God, we can begin a tradition and a heritage in our own families. If we will impart the love of God into their lives, we will see changes that affect not only our children but our children's children, to the glory of God.

Restoring the Blessing

One of the most powerful ways we are to express the heart of Father God to our children is to bless them. In Bible times, this was most clearly seen in the father's blessing of his firstborn son. Isaac's younger son, Jacob, so desired this blessing that he tricked his older brother, Esau, into giving the blessing of the firstborn to him.

When Esau realized what Jacob had done, he was left with a bitter void and craving nothing else could fill. His bitter cry is echoed by so many today: *"Bless me, even me also, O my father..."* (Genesis 27:38).

Our children cry out desperately for our approval. They cry out to know that we appreciate and accept them unconditionally. The blessing of a father is so important that many adults, who never felt their fathers' approval, spend a lifetime looking for it from others. They have an empty yearning they try to fulfill through careers, relationships and empty pursuits.

God is repairing this breach of divine order. He is the heavenly Father Who equips single mothers to minister in families where there is no husband and father. And He is showing a new generation of mighty men how to bless their families.

One aspect of the word *bless* is simply to say good about someone. It means we are to purposely open our hearts and impart the acceptance and approval that our wives and children crave.

Realize that your words carry spiritual power. With your words of love and faith you can affect your children in the same way that God's Words of love and faith affect us. Your commitments of time and interest will be a voice of blessing in your household. Your touch and loving embrace will give your family the sense of acceptance and love that they need.

Imitators of Father God

You are not alone in your quest to be the father God created you to be. He has equipped you. He has poured out His Holy Spirit to bring His mighty men to a place of valor in their most important arena—their family.

The Holy Spirit is here to help restore a

standard of godly fatherhood. No more renegade fathers. No more deserters from their positions. No more fathers who set aside covenant life and refuse to stand in the rightful place of love and authority.

Get in on the revolution, now. Reach out and rise up in the anointing He has provided for you. God in you will make you into a wonderful source of blessing to your household. He will help you overcome the obstacles and fears that have prevented you from expressing your love.

You can be a reflection of His fatherhood. You are equipped to represent His heart to your family. In Him you can do all things. Stand up in God today and confess: "I thank You, Lord, that the Anointed One and His Anointing lives in me. Because of that anointing, I will be the father I am created to be. My heart is turned toward my children, and I will train them to keep Your ways and receive their inheritance in covenant with You. I thank You that You have chosen me to represent Your heart of love to my family. I do not set aside my covenant with You or with them. And I thank You that by Your Holy Spirit I am raised up as a mighty man of valor before my family. Amen."

Chapter 8

A Word About Your Children

Gloria Copeland

"But thus saith the Lord, Even the captives of the mighty shall be taken away, and the prey of the terrible shall be delivered: for I will contend with him that contendeth with thee, and I will save thy children."
—ISAIAH 49:25

The world has much to say about your children these days—and most of it is bad. We're being told their economic futures are bleak, their ethics are waning and, for the most part, they're on a downward slide.

But if you've made Jesus Lord of your life, God has something very different to say about your children. He says they're headed for heaven, not hell, for a blessing, not a curse. So ignore the world and trust the Word. It has the power to turn your children's lives around!

"Thus saith the Lord; Refrain thy voice from weeping, and thine eyes from tears: for thy work shall be rewarded, saith the Lord; and they

[your children] shall come again from the land of the enemy. And there is hope in thine end, saith the Lord, that thy children shall come again to their own border" (Jeremiah 31:16-17).

"And all thy children shall be taught of the Lord; and great shall be the peace of thy children" (Isaiah 54:13).

"The seed of the righteous shall be delivered" (Proverbs 11:21).

"Blessed is the man that feareth the Lord, that delighteth greatly in his commandments. His seed shall be mighty upon earth: the generation of the upright shall be blessed" (Psalm 112:1-2).

"I will contend with him that contendeth with thee, and I will save thy children" (Isaiah 49:25).

"The Lord is good to all: and his tender mercies are over all his works" (Psalm 145:9).

"...I will pour my spirit upon thy seed, and my blessing upon thine offspring" (Isaiah 44:3).

"As for me, this is my covenant with them, saith the Lord; My spirit that is upon thee, and my words which I have put in thy mouth, shall not depart out of thy mouth, nor out of the mouth of thy seed, nor out of the mouth of thy seed's seed, saith the Lord, from henceforth and for ever" (Isaiah 59:21).

Giving Your Children an Inheritance of Faith

Chapter 9

Creflo A. Dollar

"And these words, which I command thee this day, shall be in thine heart: And thou shalt teach them diligently unto thy children, and shalt talk of them when thou sittest in thine house, and when thou walkest by the way, and when thou liest down, and when thou risest up."

—DEUTERONOMY 6:6-7

As a pastor and a parent, it concerns me when teenagers who have grown up in Christian homes turn their backs on God and start living like the devil. It concerns me that there are godly parents, Christian parents, who pray, tithe and serve as leaders in the church—yet their children grow up only to rebel against the faith.

According to the Bible, such a situation shouldn't even be possible because there is a scriptural law, or principle, which states, *"Train up a child in the way he should go: and when he is old, he will not depart from it"* (Proverbs 22:6).

That scripture is definite. It is spiritual fact. But it's not reality in a great many households.

Therefore, we must conclude one of two things—either God is a liar (and we know better than that!), or we are not training our children correctly.

"But Pastor Dollar," you may say, "heaven knows I'm trying! I've been trying for years to bring my children in line, but I just can't seem to figure out how to do it!"

I understand. I've had that same struggle and so have millions of other Christian parents. But it's time we stopped struggling and trying to figure things out on our own. It's time we just opened our Bibles and started putting God's laws and principles into operation in our families. It's time we started doing things God's way.

What is God's way? You can find it in Genesis 8:22. There, God tells us, *"While the earth remaineth, seedtime and harvest, and cold and heat, and summer and winter, and day and night shall not cease."*

What Seeds Are Being Planted in Your Child's Heart?

Seedtime and harvest. That is God's method of operation in everything He does. It's been His way since the beginning, and it will continue to be His way as long as this Earth remains.

Seedtime and harvest is how you were saved. The principle of seedtime and harvest is what made it possible for you to have children in the first place. You planted seed and received a harvest. And seedtime and harvest is the method you must use to raise those children.

Read Proverbs 4:20-23 and you'll see what I mean. *"My son, attend to my words; incline thine ear unto my sayings. Let them not depart from thine eyes; keep them in the midst of thine heart. For they are life unto those that find them, and health to all their flesh. Keep thy heart with all diligence; for out of it are the issues of life."*

Those verses reveal exactly how everything in life comes to us. First, something is planted like seed in the ground of our hearts. How does it get into that ground? Through the eyes, the ears and the mouth. Those three avenues are actually gateways through which things gain entrance into our hearts.

Once the seed is in the ground, it will grow and produce a harvest. If it's good seed, it will produce a good harvest. If you don't guard the ground, however, then you'll get unwanted seed on it and things will begin to grow that you don't want. But, one way or another, for better or for worse, you *will* get a harvest.

If we, as Christian parents, want to have children and teenagers who will keep the faith, we cannot neglect this system of seedtime and harvest. As parents, we are responsible for guarding the hearts of our children until they grow to the point where they can accept that responsibility themselves. We must watch over what is being planted in them because when they are young, the ground of their hearts is wide open to any and every kind of seed. And those seeds will become the forces that establish the kind of person they will grow up to be.

I don't want my daughter watching MTV, because I'm guarding her heart. I don't want her listening to lustful music, because I'm guarding her heart. I don't want those kinds of influences going in her eyes and her ears because I don't want her to grow up thinking and acting like some ungodly rap musician. I want her to grow up to be a woman of God.

Of course, guarding against unwanted seed is only part of our job as parents. We must also be planting good seed in our children's hearts. We must do what is necessary to give them an inheritance of faith that's strong enough to sustain them when they grow up.

If I want my daughters to enjoy a lifetime of victory in the Lord, I have to make sure they understand what I understand about the Word of God. I must see to it they have a revelation of how to prosper. I must be sure they know how to get healed and how to get ahead—not by depending on other people to make them successful, but by depending on faith in God.

It's much more important for me to leave an inheritance of faith to my children than it is for me to leave them a financial inheritance. If I leave them an inheritance of faith, they can get every material thing I ever had—and much more!

The New Testament tells us about one particular young man who received such an inheritance of faith. His name was Timothy, and he pastored some of the great, early churches that were started by the Apostle Paul. In 2 Timothy 1:3-5 Paul wrote to him and said:

> ...without ceasing I have remembrance of thee in my prayers night and day; Greatly desiring to see thee, being mindful of thy tears, that I may be filled with joy; When I call to remembrance the unfeigned faith that is in thee, which dwelt first in thy grandmother Lois, and thy mother Eunice; and I am persuaded that in thee also.

Timothy was in a bad situation when Paul wrote to him—but he made it through in victory, mainly because he had an inheritance of faith!

Teaching the Principles

Sadly enough, many Christian parents today aren't giving their children what Timothy's relatives provided for him. They aren't handing down their faith. The reason is simple. They just don't know how.

I can't tell you in this brief article everything you need to know about passing down your faith to your children, but I can tell you a few simple truths that will get you started—truths that have helped me greatly in recent years.

The first one is so obvious, it seems we should hardly need to say it. Yet, most of us have to admit we haven't fully incorporated it into our lives. It is this: We must take the time, not just to learn the principles of the Word ourselves, but also to teach them to our children. Deuteronomy 6:5-7 says it this way: *"Thou shalt love the Lord thy God with all thine heart, and with all thy soul, and with all thy might. And these words, which I command thee this day, shall be in thine heart: And thou shalt teach them diligently unto thy children, and shalt talk of them when thou sittest in thine house, and when thou walkest by the way, and when thou liest down, and when thou risest up."*

Notice verse 6 says the Word must be in your heart—not in your head, in your heart! You are not going to be able to impart into the lives of your children a truth you just mentally agree is true. You must have that Word living and established inside you. You must have revelation knowledge of how it works. You must have applied it and seen it produce results in your own life. Then, and only then, will you be able to explain that Word to your children in a meaningful way.

Also notice that verse says you should talk about the Word when you sit in your house. That means this is not just a Sunday ritual. You need to sit down at home and talk to your child in a practical way about the Word.

You don't have to get deep and theological about it. (Please don't!) Leave off the "thees" and "thous." Just show your child how the Word applies to him and his world.

Take advantage of the opportunities that arise when you're sitting around the table. Learn how to weave the Word of God into every conversation. For example, when your son starts telling you about all the girls he's interested in, that's an excellent opportunity to do some weaving.

You might say, "You know son, the reason we like girls so much is because God made men that way. In the very beginning, He looked at Adam and said, 'Boy, you don't need to be alone!' Then He put him to sleep, took out one of his ribs, and made a wife for him.

"My goodness, she was a masterpiece. He made her so wonderfully that when Adam woke up and saw her, he said, 'Wow! I feel good!' We still feel that way today, don't we, son? But one thing you need to remember: God just took one rib and made one woman for Adam. There weren't any spare ribs lying around, and there weren't any spare women. I want you to understand that you're destined to find that one woman God made for you...."

What have you imparted to your son through a conversation like that? You've taken away the worldly principle that says "fool around with as many women as you can," and replaced it with God's principle of marriage and faithfulness to one person. That's the way to teach the Word.

Give Them a Pattern...and Be Persistent

The second thing you must do if you want to plant good seed in the hearts of your children, and leave them with an inheritance of faith, is this: Give them a pattern. Let your life be a living example of how faith works.

Children learn more by watching what we do than by listening to what we say. You can talk the Christian talk, but if you come home and complain about your day at work, if you blame the boss and the secretary for all your problems and act like none of them is your fault, that's what your child will learn to do. Before you know it, he'll be coming home from school, blaming his teacher and his classmates for situations instead of accepting responsibility himself.

By the same token, what if you run into a difficult time at work, and you've been told you're going to be laid off? If you come home and say, "Come on, kids, let's pray. The company is cutting my job, but the Word of God says blessing and increase are mine. So let's pray and believe God is in control of our circumstances." Your children are going to learn not to panic, but to pray and trust God.

The third thing you must do to train your children in the ways of God is to be persistent. They must see you hang in there and do what needs to be done—when it's convenient and when it isn't.

There are times in all our lives when we say to ourselves, "I wish I could just break down and cry. I wish I could just forget this faith business for a few minutes and speak doubt and unbelief." But when you're tempted to do that, remember your children are watching you. They are waiting to see how you're going to respond to this situation so they'll know how to respond to it when it happens to them.

So get yourself together, and be persistent in your faith!

Participate, Give Positive Praise, and Pray

The fourth important element that's necessary if you want to impart faith to your children is participation. Something positive happens when you get involved in what concerns or interests them. Through participation, you can establish a caring relationship that makes it easier for you to communicate with them and teach them the values and life skills they need to know.

When your son comes home from school with a problem, do you think, *Here's an opportunity to participate,* or do you say, "I don't have time to mess with this, son! You handle it yourself!"

Of course, you might never say such a thing out loud—but you may well be saying it very clearly with your actions. If you don't find the time to attend your child's band concerts and school plays, if you don't take the time to talk with your child about that problem at school, to pray with him about it and visit his teacher if necessary, the message you're communicating is this—I don't care. And that is one message children never forget.

The fifth tool you can use to train up your child in the way he or she should go is positive praise. It's the greatest motivation for doing what's right.

We always seem to have time to tell children what they've done wrong. But how often do we take the time to tell them what they've done right? If you don't do that very often, make a conscious effort to start praising your children more. Purposely find five things a day you can praise them about.

When your daughter dresses up and looks pretty, for example, compliment her. Say, "Oh my, you look beautiful. You'd better watch out. You're going to walk out that door one of these days and some handsome Christian boy is going to drive by and say, 'Praise the Lord, Sugar! You're the one for me!'"

Finally, and most important of all—pray! God will honor your prayers where your children are concerned. Take time daily to pray in faith over them. Take time to declare, "The mercies of God hover over my child! My child is not going to be infected by the drug pushers. My child is going to be able to say no, because he is a disciple of the Lord, taught by Him, obedient to His Word, and great is his peace!"

Remember this: You *can* have godly children. God has promised that if you will train up your children in the way they should go, when they are old they will not depart from it. So get busy training. Get busy planting the seeds of the Word in their hearts by teaching them God's principles, setting a pattern for them, being persistent in your faith, participating with them, praising them and praying for them. Give them an inheritance of faith. They will be forever grateful!

Question & Answer: Rebellious Children

"Praise ye the Lord. Blessed is the man that feareth the Lord, that delighteth greatly in his commandments. His seed shall be mighty upon earth: the generation of the upright shall be blessed."
—PSALM 112:1-2

Kenneth
Copeland

Q: Brother Copeland, I don't know what to do about my teenage children. They're rebelling against the things of the Lord and—in spite of my prayers—they're getting deeper in trouble every day. I'm so worried about them. What should I do?

A: First of all, you must start being moved by faith. You can't get anything accomplished as long as you allow fear and worry to dominate your thinking. Stop the negative flow by starting to think and talk what the Word of God says about your children instead of dwelling on the problems you see in their lives. Isaiah 54:13, for instance, says that all your children shall be taught of the Lord, and great shall be their peace. Receive that promise for your children. Start believing it and speaking it. Then, find other promises (such as Psalm 112:1-2 and Deuteronomy 28:4) and use them to build a foundation of faith.

Gloria and I did that many years ago for our children. We saw the devil trying to get a foothold in their lives, so one weekend we got our concordance and four or five translations of the Bible. We began to search out scriptures and write out agreement prayers concerning our children.

We tore into the devil with the Word of God, and started saying "Thank God, our children are not going to hell. Thank God, they are taught of the Lord and great is their peace! Instead of walking the floor and worrying about the problem, we walked the floor and praised God for the solution.

Things didn't change instantly. We still had to go through some tough times, but the Word began to turn things around. Today my children are serving the Lord with all their hearts.

The second thing you need to do is bind the devil with the Word of God and tell him he can't have your children. Then follow the instructions

Jesus gave in Matthew 9:38: *"Pray the Lord of the harvest to send out laborers"* into the field who can reach your children.

God knows your children better than they know themselves. He knows who they'll listen to, and He knows how to bring those people into your children's lives at just the right time.

The third thing you need to do is to start rejoicing in the Lord. Zechariah 10:7-8 says, *"Those of Ephraim shall be like a mighty man, and their hearts shall rejoice as through wine. Yea their children shall see it and be glad; their heart shall rejoice in the Lord. I will hiss for them and gather them, for I have redeemed them...."*

Can you see the sequence there?

When parents get happy in the Lord, the children will see it and be glad. *Then,* God signals for them and redeems them.

Your job is to rejoice in the Lord yourself. To cast all your cares on Him. You may not even know where your children are right now. But God knows and this scripture says He will signal for them and they'll return. It doesn't matter where they are. You probably weren't exactly in your prayer closet when God first found you, were you? I know I wasn't. But He found us anyway and pulled us to Himself.

The fourth thing you need to do—and this may well be the most crucial—is this: When you're praying for your children, be sure to ask God to change you as well.

I know parents who've gone through these steps, praying that God would send their children back and He did. But when they got back home, the parents hadn't changed a bit. They jumped right in the middle of them and ran them off again.

Don't let that happen. Instead, soak your heart in the gentleness and the compassion of God. Let God turn you into someone so full of the love of Jesus and so full of His presence that your kids don't want to leave home.

Even with all this, be warned, your children may not turn around overnight. So until they do, be like Abraham and call things that be not as though they were. Say, "I'm not moved by what I see or hear. I'm not moved by what I feel. I'm moved by what I believe and I believe what God says!" Say that along with the scriptures I've outlined—not just occasionally but literally night and day. Then dig in your heels and stand. Grab hold of God's Word and refuse to let go of it where your children are concerned—and sooner or later, that Word will grab hold of them!

Chapter 11

Aim Your Child Like an Arrow

"As arrows are in the hand of a mighty man; so are children of the youth."

—PSALM 127:4

Vikki Burke

"Like arrows in the hand of a warrior, so are the children of one's youth." (New American Standard).

Those 15 words in Psalm 127:4 paint one of the most powerful portraits of parenting illustrated in the Bible. It reveals the awesome privilege God has given parents: the privilege of fashioning their children into obedient, faithful and responsible adults. God's plan and desire is that our children be trained for success—and He's called us to do it. He's called us to prepare them like a skilled craftsman fashions an arrow.

You see, God created children to win. They were born to be successful by the working of God's Word in their hearts and lives. And the word works in their hearts when parents develop and nurture a hunger for God's Word in them.

Only then can a parent truly aim them for the success God intended them to achieve.

Unfortunately, too many children have been conditioned to lose...maybe not intentionally, but they have been conditioned by a form of child abuse that gets little attention. They have become victims of neglect.

Several years ago the Duke of Windsor visited the United States and when asked what impressed him most in this country, his much-publicized response was, "The way American parents obey their children."

His comment was as tragic as it was humorous. But he described quite accurately the consequences of neglect that many children suffer.

If a parent doesn't aim a child—teach a child—to hunger and thirst after God, then the child will seek outside influences to meet the need the parent should have met. It leaves the child to raise himself and miss the mark of all that God created him to be.

You've probably seen this kind of behavior. It's all around us. It is the root of much teenage delinquency and it causes children who are not getting the attention they crave from their

parents through normal means, to get it other-
wise. It is child abuse in one of its most devastating forms.

Aim Your Child for Success

Instead of being left to flounder and fail,
constantly missing the mark of what they were
created to be, God wants children to be taught
His Word by parents who demonstrate it
moment-by-moment in their lives: *"And these
words, which I am commanding you today, shall be
on your heart; and you shall teach them diligently
to your sons and shall talk of them when you sit in
your house and when you walk by the way and
when you lie down and when you rise up"*
(Deuteronomy 6:6-7, *New American Standard*).

How important is it that we take this
command seriously? I have found the answer
in the Bible account of two fathers who acted
quite differently. Lot (Abraham's nephew)
and Noah (several generations before Lot)
faced similar circumstances and challenges in
raising their families in wicked and corrupt
generations—much like we often feel today.
Each of them had choices to make, choices

that either made them strong in aiming their children, or weak.

When put to the test, Lot failed in his choices—particularly two of them. His first mistake came when his uncle, Abraham, gave him the choice of where he wanted to live. Rather than choose a godly place, he chose to settle near Sodom, a city known for its wickedness. The Scripture says it was *"where the men were wicked and sinned against the Lord"* (see Genesis 13:5-13).

Then, he developed a tolerance for sin and hesitated to obey God, a behavior that did not impress on his family the importance of God's Word.

The Bible says that when the angels told Lot that the city of Sodom would be destroyed, *"Lot went out and spoke to his sons-in-law, who were to marry his daughters, and said, 'Up, get out of this place, for the Lord will destroy the city.' But he appeared to his sons-in-law to be jesting"* (Genesis 19:14, *New American Standard*).

Lot's family did not respond to his direction—direction he had received from God. Why would they do such a thing?

Part of the answer is in verses 15-16: *"When morning dawned, the angels urged Lot, saying, 'Up, take your wife and your two daughters, who are here, lest you be swept away in the punishment of the city.' But he hesitated. So the men seized his hand...and put him outside the city"* (New American Standard).

The failure of Lot's family to respond to his instruction should have come as no surprise. Lot himself was not quick to obey God's Word. His choices demonstrated to his children neither a hunger for God nor a respect for God's direction.

Because of these choices, his own family didn't take him seriously. Lot was more of a joke to his family than a man of integrity to be followed. Later, as Lot and his wife left the city, Lot's wife disobeyed the command to *"look not behind thee"* and was destroyed. Though spared because of Abraham's stand in covenant with God, Lot lost his wife and other family members. And he received the greatest dishonor a parent could—his family mocked his instructions and did not respect his authority.

As a parent, Lot had failed in the responsibility God made so clear to Abraham, *"For I have chosen him, in order that he may command his children...to keep the way of the Lord by doing righteousness and justice..."* (Genesis 18:19, *New American Standard*).

The Secret of Noah's Success

Generations before Lot, however, another parent, Noah, faced similar challenges and succeeded:

Noah was another who trusted God. When he heard God's warning about the future, Noah believed him even though there was then no sign of a flood, and wasting no time, he built the ark and saved his family. Noah's belief in God was in direct contrast to the sin and disbelief of the rest of the world— which refused to obey—and because of his faith he became one of those whom God has accepted (Hebrews 11:7, *The Living Bible*).

The example Noah set before his family was that he *"trusted God,"* even though there was no physical evidence to verify what he had heard. His stand of faith—trusting God for deliverance from the coming destruction—gave his children the opportunity to have his example as a pattern for their faith, and to learn to trust him as their spiritual authority.

Notice that Noah "wasted no time" in obeying God. If he had hesitated like Lot, he would have jeopardized the lives of his entire family.

Noah's faith stood in direct contrast to the rest of the world *"which refused to obey."* So, do you sometimes feel like you are the only one who believes God's Word? The only one with high standards for your children, surrounded by people whose beliefs are in direct contrast with yours? Well, you're not alone! Just keep being like Noah, who determined to obey God, regardless of what other people said or thought.

Genesis 6:8-9 says, *"But Noah found favor in the eyes of the Lord.... Noah was a righteous man, blameless in his time; Noah walked with God"* (New American Standard). Notes in the *New American Standard* version translate the word *blameless* as "complete," "perfect," or "having integrity." Noah's blameless walk apparently had a significant effect on his children. Though it had never before even rained upon the earth, they followed him in building the ark.

What brought Noah this degree of respect from his children? The kind of respect that enables a parent to properly aim a child? He committed his life to responding to God's Word, and he faithfully trained his family to do the same. Because he lived uprightly, in obedience to God, Noah's entire family was delivered from destruction. He received the greatest honor a parent could—his family respected him enough to follow his instructions.

Set Your Sights on the Word

Noah succeeded where Lot had failed—he lived a life of faith that held up God's Word as the standard. God's Word must always be the target toward which you aim your child. Regardless of the skill of the archer, if he doesn't know where the target is, he will never hit it!

All it takes to miss God's best is to fail to love Him, hear His voice and hold fast to Him: *"I call heaven and earth to witness against you today, that I have set before you life and death, the blessing and the curse. So choose life in order*

*that you may live, you and your descendants, by
loving the Lord your God, by obeying His voice,
and by holding fast to Him; for this is your life
and the length of your days..."* (Deuteronomy
30:19-20, *New American Standard*).

No one purposely lives under the curse.
But many people find themselves there by
default. *Default* means failure to do something,
or the absence of something needed. Failure of
a parent to love the Lord by obeying His voice
will expose the family to the enemy's deceptions and attacks—even if the cause is igno-
rance or indecision.

Notice how important your decision is:
"This is your life and the length of your days."
Not even God can tell you how to live. Only
you can decide that. The everyday choices you
make, and lead your children to make, last the
rest of their lives.

God's Word must always be your target.
With practice your children will learn it's not
impossible to hit the mark. Hebrews 5:14 says
that *"solid food is for the mature, who because
of practice, have their senses trained to discern
good and evil"* (*New American Standard*).

Keep your children on target by developing

in them a hunger for the solid food of the Word. Proverbs 22:6 tells us to *"train up a child in the way he should go."* The Hebrew word *train* has its origin in a word which means "palate, roof of the mouth, taste." This verse is referring to an ancient custom for weaning a child by developing his taste for solid food. According to custom, the mother would chew her food well, then put a dab of it on the palate of the child's mouth. Soon the child preferred the solid food to the milk.

In a similar way, you have been given the same responsibility regarding your child's hunger for God's Word.

So make the decision that you will take the time and effort to develop your child's palate to prefer God's ways. If you don't, that taste will be developed by others—others you probably don't prefer.

For example, the television has become a modern day baby sitter that can cultivate attitudes of rebellion and defiance. The media is doing its best to shape the thoughts of young people to adopt liberal views of sex, homosexuality, drugs and violence. They are pressing to desensitize the minds of anyone willing to absorb their filth. Don't let the television raise your child.

And avoid letting your children spend the majority of their time with other children. This serves only to reinforce the foolishness bound in their hearts (Proverbs 22:15). *"He who walks with wise men will be wise, but the companion of fools will suffer harm"* (Proverbs 13:20, *New American Standard*). Your children need your help in uprooting foolishness and replacing it with wisdom. They need time with you, listening to you, receiving your counsel and advice on matters in their lives.

Keep Your Child on Target

Aiming your child like an arrow is a conscious, willful act. Look again at Deuteronomy 6:7: *"...You shall teach [these words] diligently to your sons and shall talk of them when you sit in your house and when you walk by the way and when you lie down and when you rise up"* (*New American Standard*).

Diligence. It's a decision backed by a commitment to hold fast to that decision. Making the firm commitment to teach your children *"when you walk (or drive!) by the way, when you lie down, when you rise up"* simply means making the most of every conversation.

Just because you're a Christian and attend church faithfully does not guarantee your children are being taught your values. You cannot expect your children to get the direction they need from a couple of hours a week in church. The primary responsibility of aiming your children does not belong to the church. It belongs to you. Aim them at God's Word, then be certain to check them at regular intervals to be certain they are still pointing in the right direction.

Let everyday situations become teaching times. Be open and responsive to the Holy Spirit to use these situations, not in a condemning way, but in an encouraging, uplifting manner. God alone knows the motivation of your child's heart, and He alone can reveal to you the most effective way to reach him or her. As the Scripture says, "...*Don't keep on scolding and nagging your children, making them angry and resentful. Rather, bring them up with the loving discipline the Lord himself approves, with suggestions and godly advice*" (Ephesians 6:4, *The Living Bible*).

Be certain your children are aware of your availability, no matter what you're doing. They should know they are most important to you, and you will stop anything to meet their need.

Make it a practice to talk about the Word in all your activities. When you take a walk or go to the park, use that time to develop an appreciation for God's creation, the birds, the beauty of the trees, the wild flowers, even the clouds in the sky.

Another opportunity for ministering the Word is bedtime. This is an especially powerful time to deposit into your children. They may have a special need for your comfort, love and approval, encouragement, assurance, or just a listening ear. The words you speak before bed last all night and are there first thing in the morning.

Using a fun, casual atmosphere, you can be very effective in impressing powerful truths to your children. As a family we frequently tell the stories about how God delivered us from Satan's grip; how He rescued us from a particular situation; even how God brought Dennis and me together to be married; and how God miraculously gave us a child when medically it was impossible. In this way, our daughter can grow to see God's Word as part of our everyday experience.

Shoot for Life, Not Just a Lifestyle

If your children are not to be drawn off target as they grow, they will need to see Christianity as not merely a lifestyle, but as life itself! Reach beyond the limitations of the mental realm and communicate with the hearts of your children.

What have you trained your children to prefer? Have they developed a taste for the things of the world, or the things of God? Determine to model your life in such a way that it makes growing up something worth attaining.

Children learn by example. Impart wisdom to your children through your companionship. Cultivate and nurture friendship with them.

If you aim your child like the warrior would aim the weapon in his hand, you will not be ashamed. Your meaningful relationship with your children will cause them to see the truth and appreciate your wise counsel. And the joys of living in the promises of God's Word will bless them through eternity.

Parent, Be the Anointed Plugger-Upper!

Chapter 12

"He who spares his rod [of discipline] hates his son, but he who loves him disciplines diligently and punishes him early."

—PROVERBS 13:24,
(THE AMPLIFIED BIBLE)

Ian Britza

Escape artists...I've been fascinated by them for years. Performers like the late Harry Houdini have amazed many people for decades using techniques and illusion to convince the crowds they had found the hidden way out of seemingly immovable constraints.

But it's not these escape artists who capture my attention the most. No, my interest is in the real pros—the ones who without tricks or illusion find their way out of air-tight situations in no time. These outstanding masters of escape search and probe and test relentlessly to find the weak link or loophole that will free them of their constraints. These are really the world's great escape artists. And they live right under our noses!

You know who I'm talking about? The escape

skills of our children are highly advanced! They can smell a loophole miles away. If they can find a way out from correction, they will smell it and go for it.

So what does a parent do to bridle the escape artists? We have to be anointed "plugger-uppers." We have to plug up our own loopholes of deceived attitudes and wrong actions that provide our children an escape from the loving, positive, Bible correction they need. Read on and I'll show you what I mean...

Plug Up the Loophole of Humanism

The first loophole you'll need to plug as a parent is any humanistic thinking on your part. With its rejection of the supernatural and emphasis on using reason to discover self-worth and identity, humanism has caused some parents to conclude that only by leaving children to themselves will they be happy and fulfilled. Humanistic thinking teaches that parental authority and correction are wrong and only hinder the true freedom of the child.

But you don't have to go to a university or be a rocket scientist to know that if you leave your child by himself, he's going to end up in trouble. That's why it's not when your child is making noise that you get concerned. It's when he's quiet that your ears perk up!

Children left to themselves don't produce actions that will make them happy and fulfilled and truly free later in life. Instead of true fulfillment and wisdom being bound up in the heart of a child, Proverbs 22:15 says, *"Foolishness is bound in the heart of a child; but the rod of correction shall drive it far from him."* I don't care how cute your little one is, he does not need to be left alone to do his own thing. He needs (and wants) your loving, biblical correction and guidance.

Plug Up the Loophole of False Love

Many parents leave loopholes in the correcting of their children. They fail to understand the real meaning of the word *love* so they "go soft." Proverbs 13:24 says, *"He who spares his rod [of discipline] hates his son, but he who loves him diligently disciplines and punishes him early"* (The Amplified Bible).

Some parents really have trouble with that.

They say, "Well, I love my children too much to spank them." On the surface this sounds good. But this is a false love that falls short of the kind of love God wants parents to show to their children. It's a deceived mind-set that falls prey to this false love.

You see, without true love, there really is no true correction. Hebrews 12:6 says, *"For the Lord corrects and disciplines every one whom He loves, and He punishes, even scourges, every son whom He accepts and welcomes to His heart and cherishes"* (The Amplified Bible).

I used to think I surely must hold the record for being in the pastor's office the most for correction. I don't know how many times I heard these words, "You know, Ian, it's a joy correcting you."

"Thanks," I said. (It may have been a joy to him, but I usually wasn't feeling so joyful at the time!)

"You know why?" he would continue. "Because I know that you know we love you. And because you know and I know that we love you, when we tell you what needs to be changed, we know you'll do it."

True love is God's love. It's the kind of love that desires the best and highest for every individual. To let foolishness or anything else stand between a child and God's best for his life is not true love.

Plug the Loophole of Neglect

The rampant child abuse of our day is another major hindrance to proper correction. There are different kinds of abuse—sexual, verbal, physical and emotional—and they are all horrible.

But let me suggest another form of abuse that people often overlook—neglect. It is the failure to provide loving correction, as we're instructed in the Word. Proverbs 23:13 says, *"Do not withhold discipline from a child; if you punish him with the rod, he will not die" (New International Version).*

That word "punish" does not mean punching or thrashing or knocking a child around. It means to hit with a reed-like instrument. Perhaps the closest thing to it is a piece of cane with the end burned so that it is smooth—something flexible enough to sting, but not to injure.

Don't use a paddle made of wood that is

115

not flexible and can possibly injure a child. And don't use your hands to smack your child. Remember, your hands are made to love, not to correct.

The point is that you want to start young enough with your children so they learn that you give them correction because you love them. You want them to learn to receive correction and learn the value of obeying promptly.

Plug Up the Loophole of Laziness

As important as the proper use of the rod is, there is much more to positive correction than the sting of a spanking. Positive, Bible correction. It takes time—time to make sure the child understands what he or she has done wrong, and time for repentance and restoration.

This means parents must plug the loophole of laziness in their own lives. The reason we often don't like to correct our children is because we're so busy. We're always in the middle of something when the need for correction arises. We want to speed through the correction and get it over with quickly.

But true correction cannot be done quickly,

because it is not punishment. It is ministry to the soul of the child—and each child is different. When my son Timothy was much younger, he usually knew when he had done wrong. He would just say, "Hey, I know" and receive his correction. But his brother, Michael, always had a defense. You had to take the time to prove to him that he had gone against God's Word. Once you had done that, then he submitted.

It takes time to make sure your child knows he or she has sinned. It also takes time to make sure they have received the correction in their hearts. Don't let a child go back to playing with a bad attitude. Make sure they've truly understood. I test this by having them hug me after I correct them. If they hug me like a sack of potatoes, I spend more time with the correction, I remind them that I love them and look for them to receive the correction. A child who does not receive the correction in his heart has not been trained in anything. Nothing eternal has been imparted into his life—nothing that will help him succeed in life as a Christian and as a contributor to society.

I taught my children that once we deal with the correction, it is finished. When our relationship is back together and we go outside that bedroom door, I'm not holding anything against them and they are not holding anything against me. That's why their hug is so important.

Plug the Loophole of Multiple Warnings

Parents can also fall into the trap of taking action only after issuing continual warnings, or after reaching the point of personal anger or frustration. The reason so many children don't obey until their parents have asked them four or five times, or until their parents become angry and threaten them, is that they have been trained to wait until then.

Children learn quickly when their parents really mean what they say. They will transfer that to their relationship with God. If they have been trained to delay being obedient to God, they'll only listen to God when they're in trouble, without money, sick and at the point of death. If they are trained to expect several warnings, they will learn to ignore God's first instruction. What if that instruction was to keep them from a life-threatening situation?

There may be no second opportunity. It pays to hear the first time.

By enforcing prompt obedience, we train our children to hear God's voice. Children should learn that their parents mean what they say, and that their parents expect them to obey the first time they give an instruction.

Plug Up the Loophole of Excuses

Parents use a number of excuses for not disciplining their children. Some of the following may be familiar to you. All of them are loopholes that can keep your child from receiving the kind of consistent, loving correction that will bring positive results in their lives...

1. *My little blessings aren't old enough to understand.* If a child is old enough to know the words "doggie, bye-bye, da-da, no-no," he's old enough to understand. As cute as our children are, they still have a sin nature. As parents, we must address this and discipine our children.

2. *He's tired today. He's always naughty when he is tired.* It's remarkable that two minutes before the child disobeys, he's not

tired. Even though a child may be tired, he can learn to behave and watch his attitude. Children need to be guided, molded and taught how to behave properly.

3. *But it isn't his fault.* This puts the blame for your child's obnoxious behavior on the child he was playing with. Are we going to say Johnny learned to lie from Peter, therefore it isn't Johnny's fault? Even though children are around others who may show poor behavior, parents must still require proper behavior from their children. Children need to learn that the fact everyone else is doing it doesn't make it right.

4. *He's the way he is because we're not at home.* I'm sure we've all used this one somewhere along the way. It sounds good when we're saying it. But it can't be an excuse.

You are your child's security. Your word is to be obeyed whether you are at the shopping center or at the zoo. Once I was messing around on the back pew while my father was preaching. He stopped in the middle of his sermon and announced, "I'm going to have to get down from the pulpit." He walked to my row, pulled me out, took me outside, gave me a wallop, then sat me next to my mother. When he returned to the pulpit, he announced, "I lead by example." A few other parents took their children out and gave them a wallop.

5. *He's not feeling well.* If a child is very sick, he'll be too sick to be naughty. You know when your child is naughty and when your child is sick. If they are naughty, they are not that sick. Even when you are sick, if you have been trained, you will still be doing the Word.

6. *He's just like his uncle. His uncle has a real temper, too.* You don't sit still and let every bad hereditary trait manifest in the life of your child, so don't put up with this excuse either. The power of God's love and deliverance working through your loving correction will deal with those hereditary traits.

7. *He'll just outgrow it.* Maybe so. But he won't outgrow the attitudes associated with that disobedience. Children whose parents let them develop wrong attitudes will take those attitudes right up into their teenage and adult years.

Plugged Loopholes Yield Big Blessings

It takes great strength for parents to plug the loopholes of correction. Don't let anyone tell you that it's easy. It takes the greatest strength of your Christian nature to know how to correct your children when they're young.

Don't be fooled by those little cries and those cute little blue eyes that look at you— those cries and looks that would cause you to stop and to put correction aside. And make no mistake, your children know just which of your buttons to push. They know how to turn you on and how to turn you off. If you love your child, you'll not be swayed by outward emotions.

Remember, real love chooses the best. That is why it must bring correction to anything within your child's life that will keep him from the best. If you really love God, and you really love your child, you will do everything in your power to correct him. And you will start by teaching your child early that correction is an expression of love.

Now, this is completely opposite the philosophy of the world. That's why it's so difficult. It's easy to do what the world says to do. It always takes faith to do what God's Word says to do. It takes faith to plug the loopholes. But the results are worth it, and your children will thank you for it.

Chapter 13

A Discipline That Blesses

"Correct thy son, and he shall give thee rest; yea, he shall give delight unto thy soul."

—Proverbs 29:17

Willie George

What is the best gift you can give your children in troubled times?

Without a doubt I believe it is godly character. A sensitive spirit and persevering character will steer your children through anything troubled times can throw at them.

The discipline to develop godly character will not always be convenient or comfortable for you or them. But if you will commit yourself to scriptural discipline, your children will honor and bless you and they in turn will be blessed with godly character and long lives.

Proverbs 29:17 promised that if you *"correct thy son...he will give thee rest; yea, he shall give delight unto thy soul."* This is not stating a possibility. It's a fact.

Your discipline gives your children the opportunity to honor and obey you, which opens the door to blessings for them. Ephesians 6:1-3 says, *"Children, obey your parents in the Lord: for this is right. Honour thy father and mother; which is the first commandment with promise; That it may be well with thee, and thou mayest live long on the earth."*

A Job Well Done

First, discipline that blesses will teach your children to be responsible—how to work, how to finish a job and how to handle money. There is an old Jewish proverb that says, "If you don't teach your child a trade, its the same as if you taught him to steal."

A child can pick up a lot of things naturally. But you probably know by now that work is not one of them. It shouldn't surprise you, then, that training your child to do a job well will be harder work for you than for them. You have to stay with them if you are going to establish the standard.

You may think, *Staying with them takes too much time. I could do this quicker myself.* But you are not doing your children any favors by not letting them finish the job right.

One of our sons went through a time when he

would not get his schoolwork done. He came home with bad papers. We spanked. We scolded. We told him to do his homework. But nothing worked.

Finally, we made the commitment to inspect every lesson, lesson by lesson. It was as much work for us as it was for him! But we stuck with it until we developed a habit in him.

No quick fix could bring out the right behavior. No drastic shock treatment was called for. What he needed was his parents to be committed to staying with him, watching over his work and making him give an account.

Your children need you to stay with them until they have finished a project—whether it be a chore, a school assignment or sticking out baseball season. You need to inspect the finished work and be ready to commend them when it is done correctly. When it's not, show them how to do it right and have them go at it again. Don't let them give up. Teach your children how to derive satisfaction from a job well done.

Another responsibility your children need to be taught is how to handle money. If you don't want money to control your children, then you need to teach your children to control money. Don't give them a lot of money to spend foolishly. Teach them how to earn it, save it and tithe it.

Tithing will teach them how to manage their finances—it will bring wisdom in handling money.

Character Praised

Second, discipline that blesses exalts character. All of us love to praise our little children when they sing pretty, recite poetry and look cute or handsome in their dress-up clothes.

But as they grow older, they need praise for their character—not just their God-given talents and abilities.

You can do this in some simple ways. For instance, you can clap just as enthusiastically when your son returns from carrying out the trash as you did when he hit a home run.

Impress on your children that the winners in life are those who have the most character. Then even when they have been unfairly treated, they will stick to their goals. They will wind up on top of the heap when everyone else has quit.

A lot of reason God has allowed me the impact and ministry I have with kids today is that I don't know how to quit—something I never picked up naturally.

I went to live with my uncle as a rebellious 17-year-old. He put me to work and made me finish every job. And he inspected everything I did.

To get me through college, he and I got into the hay-hauling business. It developed character I never had. We went to work earlier, stayed later and stacked our hay higher than the competition.

I wanted to quit, but my uncle wouldn't let me. Eventually I developed such satisfaction out of doing a job well that if my uncle had to leave for an emergency, I'd go ahead and finish hauling the hay myself.

That helped me later in life with projects and goals such as the *Gospel Bill Show*. I didn't meet with instant success. It seemed that nobody wanted to help us. We'd sent out tapes and nobody returned our calls. Even my own kids didn't respond well to the show. They saw it once but didn't want to watch it again! The lack of response was almost discouraging.

But I knew what God said and I didn't quit. The teaching not to quit put me over. Many people don't have that quality in their lives because nobody ever pushed them and drove them to finish.

Abundant Hugs

Third, discipline that blesses you and your children will involve lots of hugs. Show your children affection. Let them know you love them whether they perform well or not. They should not have to earn your love based on their successes or failures.

Demonstrate your love. Hug your kids. And that includes your boys. It's not true that hugging is a sign of sissiness and that it's not masculine to hug your boys. Boys need hugs, too. If you'll give your kids the love and affection they need at home, you'll prevent them from desiring to go find it in the world. A lot of young girls are willing to give their bodies over to some boy before marriage because they're looking for the affection and hugs their daddies never gave them. A lot of teenage boys are looking for the kind of commitment out of a girl that only a future wife can give because they don't get affection at home.

I've hugged my kids so much, that when I walk in the door all three of them will run to hug daddy. One of my sons even stops playing his video game sometimes to do it. Now, when he stops playing a video game, you know he's expressing affection!

Loving Correction

The fourth thing you need to do if your discipline is going to bless you and your children is to correct them when they rebel. This is not punishment. Criminals, you punish. Children, you correct.

Correction should be in proportion to the infraction and appropriate to the age of the child. You don't beat a baby's bottom with a fine board. Nor will swats convince an 18-year-old he shouldn't have stayed out past curfew.

Find what speaks to each child. You might have to put up with a little crying from a baby who doesn't want to go to bed. Or the car and dating privileges may have to be taken away from a disobedient teenager.

In the in-between ages, where they are old enough to correct with a rod, remember that training with a rod is scriptural. Proverbs 13:24 says that *"he that spareth his rod hateth his son: but he that loveth him chasteneth him betimes."* Of course, you don't hate your children, but if you refuse to correct them, it will have the same impact on them as if you did.

Your correction should not be given in anger. Proverbs 22:8 says, *"He that soweth iniquity shall reap vanity: and the rod of anger shall fail."* If your child gets the spanking strictly because you're angry, he'll begin to think that every time he gets a spanking it's because you're mad and not because he's done wrong. He will relate correction, not to his behavior, but to your attitude.

Discipline will not be fun for you or your child, but it will yield peace. Hebrews 12:11 says, *"Now no chastening for the present seemeth to be joyous, but grievous: nevertheless afterward it yieldeth the peaceable fruit of righteousness unto them which are exercised thereby."*

What you want to do is create a sensitive spirit in your child. You want your children to be bothered when they do something wrong. You'll know you're doing well when they've done something and can't hide it.

This won't happen overnight. It will require consistency. It will require a commitment. But the rewards are great. Never forget: Your partnership with God will always help you to train up your children in troubled times. With God, you will succeed!

Prayer for Salvation and Baptism in the Holy Spirit

Heavenly Father, I come to You in the Name of Jesus. Your Word says, "Whosoever shall call on the name of the Lord shall be saved" (Acts 2:21). I am calling on You. I pray and ask Jesus to come into my heart and be Lord over my life according to Romans 10:9-10: "If thou shalt confess with thy mouth the Lord Jesus, and shalt believe in thine heart that God hath raised him from the dead, thou shalt be saved. For with the heart man believeth unto righteousness; and with the mouth confession is made unto salvation." I do that now. I confess that Jesus is Lord, and I believe in my heart that God raised Him from the dead.

I am now reborn! I am a Christian—a child of Almighty God! I am saved! You also said in Your Word, "If ye then, being evil, know how to give good gifts unto your children: HOW MUCH MORE shall your heavenly Father give the Holy Spirit to them that ask him?" (Luke 11:13). I'm also asking You to fill me with the Holy Spirit. Holy Spirit, rise up within me as I praise God. I fully expect to speak with other tongues as You give me the utterance (Acts 2:4). In Jesus' Name. Amen!

Begin to praise God for filling you with the Holy Spirit. Speak those words and syllables you receive—not in your own language, but the language given to you by the Holy Spirit. You have to use your own voice. God will not force you to speak. Don't be concerned with how it sounds. It is a heavenly language!

Continue with the blessing God has given you and pray in the spirit every day.

You are a born-again, Spirit-filled believer. You'll never be the same!

Find a good church that boldly preaches God's Word and obeys it. Become part of a church family who will love and care for you as you love and care for them.

We need to be connected to each other. It increases our strength in God. It's God's plan for us.

Make it a habit to watch the *Believer's Voice of Victory* television broadcast and become a doer of the Word, who is blessed in his doing (James 1:22-25).

When The LORD first spoke to Kenneth and Gloria Copeland about starting the *Believer's Voice of Victory* magazine...

He said: *This is your seed. Give it to everyone who ever responds to your ministry, and don't ever allow anyone to pay for a subscription!*

For more than 40 years, it has been the joy of Kenneth Copeland Ministries to bring the good news to believers. Readers enjoy teaching from ministers who write from lives of living contact with God, and testimonies from believers experiencing victory through God's Word in their everyday lives.

Today, the *BVOV* magazine is mailed monthly, bringing encouragement and blessing to believers around the world. Many even use it as a ministry tool, passing it on to others who desire to know Jesus and grow in their faith!

Request your FREE subscription to the
***Believer's Voice of Victory* magazine today!**

Go to **freevictory.com** to subscribe online, or call us
1-800-600-7395 (U.S. only) or **+1-817-852-6000**.

We're Here for You!®

Our growth in God's WORD and victory in Jesus are at the very center of our hearts. In every way God has equipped us, we will help you deal with the issues facing you, so you can be the **victorious overcomer** He has planned for you to be.

The mission of Kenneth Copeland Ministries is about all of us growing and going together. Our prayer is that you will take full advantage of all the LORD has given us to share with you.

Wherever you are in the world, you can watch the *Believer's Voice of Victory* broadcast on television (check your local listings), the Internet at kcm.org or on our digital Roku channel.

Our website, **kcm.org,** gives you access to every resource we've developed for your victory. And, you can find contact information for our international offices in Africa, Asia, Australia, Canada, Europe, Ukraine and our headquarters in the United States.

Each office is staffed with devoted men and women, ready to serve and pray with you. You can contact the worldwide office nearest you for assistance, and you can call us for prayer at our U.S. number, +1-817-852-6000, 24 hours every day!

We encourage you to connect with us often and let us be part of your everyday walk of faith!

Jesus Is LORD!

Kenneth & Gloria Copeland

Kenneth and Gloria Copeland